THE BIG DITCH

The Manchester Ship Canal Seen Through The Camera Of
JOHN DARWELL

Formal opening ceremony of Manchester Ship Canal 21st May 1894.

I trust Manchester may never cease to be prosperous and thrive, and that all classes and subjects may share in the benefits attending on the success of this most important enterprise.
Queen Victoria

Published with assistance from the Arts Council of Great Britain.

Published by Countryside Publications Limited, School Lane, Brinscall, Chorley, Lancashire.
Text © John Darwell, 1987.
Printed by Tamley-Reed Limited.
ISBN 0 86157 250 5

INTRODUCTION

When I began the project of photographing the Manchester Ship Canal early in 1984, the sheer immensity and diversity of the canal was something that had completely failed to impress itself on me. This soon changed and the canal developed into an obsession that still remains. Shortly after beginning the project it was announced that the upper reaches of the canal were *uneconomic* and would close in approximately two years time? Today the future of the canal is still unknown. With this in mind I felt my photographs should try to capture the *spirit* of the canal as it awaits its future. I felt that there were enough photographs detailing the make and number of every tug boat that had ever sailed through Eastham Lock and it was with the everyday life of the waterway that I concerned myself; not only the landscape through which it passes from the dereliction of Salford Docks (now involved in a major re-development scheme) but to the beauty and relative quietude of the Mersey Estuary - if you discount the gale force wind that invariably made an appearance when I was there!

A lot of my time was spent talking to and photographing the men who, in some cases, had been involved with the canal for forty years; whose working lives revolved around the canal, the boat crews, swingbridge operators and lock crews, without whom the canal would cease to function. It is these characters both old and young that I feel reflect the canal at its most intimate; in the companionship gained by people spending their working lives in a partnership whether on a diving boat or a swingbridge tower.

I would like to express my gratitude for the innumerable cups of tea provided and for the wonderful stories told to me relating to the canal - most of which couldn't be repeated in delicate company! I apologise to all the people I met who are not included.

My eternal thanks go to David Hastie of the Ship Canal Company's Public Relations Office for all his help, and also a special thanks to Dave Watt for his advice.

I hope the photographs have managed to capture some of the essence of power and scale of this monumental engineering achievement and that the canal will have many more useful years left to run.

John Darwell

River Irwell becomes Ship Canal, Regent Road, Salford.

View across No. 2 berth, Pomona Dock.

View from canal bank to Regent Road.

Pomona Dock, Colgate Palmolive.

Manchester Docks. In the 1950s and 60s the Port of Manchester was the third major British port after London and Liverpool. 3,700 dockers handled over 16 million tonnes of cargo annually. The original docklands covered an area of over 700 acres with 5 miles of quays; No. 9 dock was the longest, at over half a mile in length. The docks and canal were designed to carry ships of 12,500 tonnes, which were the largest ocean-going vessels of the day.

Looking from Trafford Wharf to No. 9 dock, now largely demolished.

Trafford Wharf, former drydock, now used as ship breakers' yard.

Former Manchester Dry dock, now used by dismantlers. Russian fishing vessel waiting to be broken up.

Disused washroom, Salford Docks, now demolished.

During the war a ship carrying whale oil shed its load into the canal forming a crust over the water. Boats working like ice breakers were paid £8 a day to clear it.   From Mode Wheel

Tug boat Salford Docks with Russian fishing vessel.

Sludge boat docking at Weaste Wharf.

Looking towards Weaste Wharf from Mode Wheel Locks.

Vincent Costello and Pete Tarpay. Sludge boat 47 (Dangerboat).

C.P.C. Wharf and Proctor and Gamble Ltd from Eccles New Road bank.

John Greaves, swingbridge operator, Barton Bridge.

Towards M63 high level bridge, built to allow large ships to pass under, with swing bridge opening.

Beneath Barton Bridge operations tower.

Pete Dinsdale, Chief Lockmaster, Barton Locks.

Graffitti - Weston Point Dock.

Disused jetty near Barton Locks.

Downstream from Barton Locks, divers regularly inspect locks for signs of wear and removal of any debris brought down the canal.

Roy Sherratt, ferryman, Hulmes Bridge Ferry, Irlam. Operated as a free service by Ship Canal Co.

Crossing Irlam Locks, a well trodden pathway between Irlam and Flixton.

Sludge boat leaving Irlam docks, Irlam Viaduct at rear.

Sludge boat with tug, Irlam Locks.

Roy Sherratt, ferryman Hulmes Bridge.

Partington Basin is used for the loading and unloading of low and high flash products for Shell Chemicals, Shell Mex and British Gas.
It was formerly used as a loading site for coal from Lancashire, Derbyshire and Staffordshire coal fields; the coal chutes now stand idle.

Carrington Power Station and Mersey Weir, where River Mersey joins the Ship Canal for four miles before leaving again at Rixton Junction.

Looking across Partington oil basin towards Carrington.

Bobs Lane Ferry, run by Greater Manchester Transport at 10p per crossing.

Sludge boat and tug, Bobs Lane Canal needs constant dredging to prevent build up of silt carried down by the Irwell.

Oil coaster travelling from Partington Basin passing beneath Warburton Bridge.

Woolston deposit grounds where silt from the canal is pumped onto the fields forming vast tracts of rich mud. This area is now classed as a nature reserve and is set to receive recognition as Area of Special Scientific Interest. Photo taken from M6 bridge embankment.

Work/storeroom, Latchford.

Coaster approaching Latchford, viewed from Latchford Viaduct, M6 bridge seen in distance.

Ernie and Tommy, swing bridge operators, Knutsford Road.

Ian and Gary, control room, Chester Road swing bridge.

Les, Stan and Tommy, control room, Northwich Road swing bridge.

Moore as in Moore Lane Swing Bridge spelt with an 'e' eg MOORE LANE.

Since these photographs were taken the bridges have become automated 'one man'
operations.

Peter, swing bridge engineer, Moore Lane.

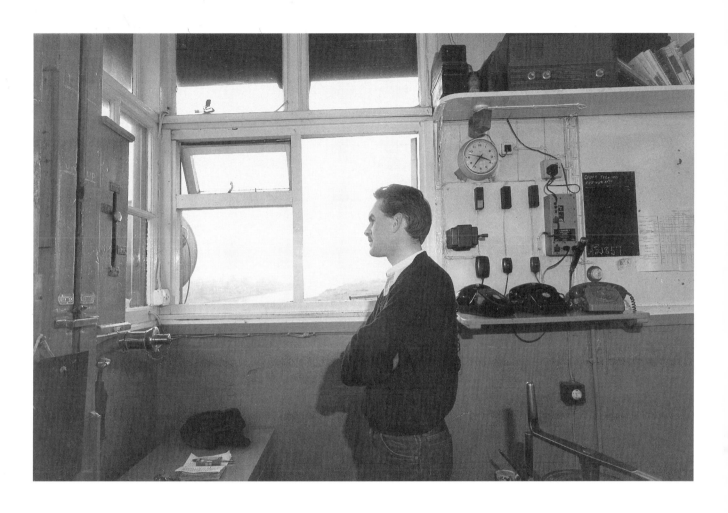

Tommy, swing bridge operator, Moore Lane.

Runcorn - Widnes Bridge. One of the largest single spans in Europe. Stands 80 feet above normal water level.

This is the best place to live, all the acid rain from over there goes over my head and lands on someone else.
                                        Jock, sole householder, Randle Sluices.

Tony Collins, swing bridge operator, Old Quay.

Mersey Estuary from Old Quay.

The gates stay here, the 250-ton floating crane has been blacked; they're afraid if it comes up here from Salford the company won't let it go back.   Lock repairman Runcorn

Runcorn-Widnes bridge from Old Quay workshops.

Ship Canal wall from beneath Runcorn-Widnes bridge.

Runcorn Docks. One of the busiest areas along the canal, with a history of handling dry bulk materials for glass-making, pottery and insulation industries.

Runcorn Docks.

Weston Point Dock, now disused.

Christ Church, Weston Point, reputedly the only church in Europe to stand on an uninhabited island (when lock gates are open). It still has its own congregation.

Weston Point.

Weaver navigation looking towards ICI from Weston Point.

Weaver Sluices. 10 sluices, each 30 feet wide, are used to control water levels along Ship Canal and Weaver Navigation by emptying excess into the Mersey Estuary. The only access to the sluices is by boat and two men work each shift of 8 hours.

Frodsham Score, only occupants sheep and rabbits. Farmers reputed to have lost up to 100 sheep in a night through drowning on the mud flats and also by washes from boats on canal.

Stanlow Oil Refinery, Ellesmere Port.

Stanlow Island.

Stanlow Oil Refinery. Two oil docks are situated on an 'island' between the Ship Canal and the Mersey Estuary and are used for the discharging of petroleum spirits.
The only access to the island is by ferryboat across the canal.

Stanlow point with disused light house, used by navigators along Mersey Estuary, with view to Mt. Manistry in distance.

Looking towards Ellesmere Port from Mt. Manistry, including disused beacon tower.

North West Water boat (Gilbert Fowler?) travelling from Eastham Locks.

I can remember a time when four ships at once were berthed here, and as one left another would immediately replace it.   Dock worker, QE11 Dock.

Ted with torch, Eastham Locks. Engineering shop.

Eric and Ralph, divers, Eastham Locks. Eric was first diver to work in QEII Dock.

George, engineering Dept Eastham Locks.

Operating lock gates joining Ship Canal to the Mersey Estuary.

End of the line, view across Mersey to Liverpool.